Turning Conflict
-into-
Intimacy

Renewing your Relationship: A Workbook for Turning Conflict Into Intimacy
Copyright © 2018 by Erin Belanger Freeh & David Olsen

All rights reserved. No part of this book may be used or reproduced in any form, electronic or mechanical, including photocopying, recording, or scanning into any information storage and retrieval system, without written permission from the author except in the case of brief quotation embodied in critical articles and reviews.

Book design by Jessika Hazelton
The Troy Book Makers • Troy, New York • thetroybookmakers.com
Printed in the United States of America

To order additional copies of this title,
contact your favorite local bookstore
or visit www.shoptbmbooks.com

ISBN: 978-1-61468-458-9

RENEWING YOUR RELATIONSHIP
— A WORKBOOK FOR —

Turning Conflict -into- Intimacy

ERIN BELANGER FREEH, LMHC
DAVID OLSEN, PHD, LCSW, LMFT

Contents

Introduction:
Healthy Conflict Resolution = Greater Intimacy 1

Chapter 1:
Why Are We Fighting?
I Thought We Were In Love! 3

    How Do We Make Sense of Conflict? 3
    The Problem is that You are
    Probably Focusing on the Wrong Problem 5
    The Problem of Regulating
    Closeness and Distance 6
    The Problem of Emotional Systems 10
    The Problem Goes Deeper 13
    Summary 17
    Questions for Reflection 17

Chapter 2:
Conflict Styles that Prevent Intimacy 21

    The Conflict-Avoidant Couple 21
    The Rapid Escalator Couple 24
    The Partner Who
    Gives Up Self to Avoid Conflict 25
    The Passive Aggressive Partner 27
    The Fight/Withdraw Combination Couple 28
    What Is Your "Fighting Style"? 29
    Questions for Reflection 29

Chapter 3:
Breaking Your Conflict Pattern 33
- Step 1: Identifying Your Pattern of Conflict. 34
- Step 2: Learning and Understanding Your Conflict Map. 37
- Questions for Reflection 46

Chapter 4:
Beginning to Make Change:
From Conflict to Greater Intimacy 49
- Healthy Conflict Must Start Slow. 50
- Ground Rules for Conflict 55
- Making Effective Repair 56
- Questions for Reflection 57

Chapter 5:
Making Real Lasting Change 59
- Five Blocks to Making Lasting Progress. 59
- Summary 68

Suggested Readings. 70

Introduction:
Healthy Conflict Resolution = Greater Intimacy

We've all heard the saying, "Happy wife, happy life", and maybe we've even bought into the belief that making our spouse happy is the key to a happy marriage. While it might sound counterintuitive, healthy conflict is actually a necessary part of all relationships – in fact, it is a key component in building intimacy. If we work to minimize or prevent conflict, we also work to minimize or prevent intimacy. In much the same vein, however, if conflict takes over the relationship, there is no room for healthy intimacy.

Understanding and being able to work on healthier conflict management is essential to growth as a couple and to building intimacy together. Most couples, though, have great difficulty working through conflict, and some even work hard to avoid it. This is largely because couples frequently do not understand the origins of their conflict. Instead, they come to simplistic solutions thinking that they are arguing about a single topic like money, or parenting, or sex. In reality, conflict goes far deeper and is rooted in more complicated issues. Without understanding those issues, and the ways they manifest in conflict, couples will find little success with building a more intimate relationship.

This book, the follow-up to *Renewing your Relationship: 5 Necessary Steps,* (Olsen and Berlanger-Freeh, 2017) will first explore the deeper sources of conflict in relationships, and how to begin to understand the origins of that conflict. It will then introduce you to common conflict styles that prevent intimacy. Next, it will begin to explore the skills needed to engage in healthy conflict, and what gets in the way of us using those skills. Finally, we will delve into the core of how to develop healthy conflict and deeper intimacy by providing a series of very practical steps for resolving conflict.

Chapter 1:
Why Are We Fighting? I Thought We Were In Love!

How Do We Make Sense of Conflict?

On the way to a couples therapy conference, my Uber driver began to tell me about his relationship problems. After talking for a while, he asked a profound question: why do so many couples have so much difficulty, and what is underneath all that conflict? Great question! Before describing styles of conflict and how to do conflict better, it helps to understand the deeper origins of conflict. Knowing what drives deep conflict and causes such deep pain and division is a necessary first step.

In the beginning stages of a relationship, as a couple thinks about getting married and spending their lives together, no one thinks they will have much marital conflict, especially in the excitement and expectation of planning their weddings! In fact, in the early falling in love stage, conflict is largely missing. Couples, even in the midst of intense conflict, fondly recall their early days when they were dating. They describe easy conversations, lots of fun together, strong physical attraction, and enjoying lots of time together. In fact, in premarital counseling many couples have difficulty even thinking about where they will have significant conflict. Not surprisingly, couples are confused by the source of their conflict and often resort to simplistic explanations that suggest that the other has somehow changed. "He used to talk more, now he just watches ESPN", "She now has to call her mother everyday", "we used to have great sex, but now it is boring and routine", "it seems like we can't resolve anything without a blowout argument". The list of complaints goes on and on. Both partners are confused about what is driving the conflict and too often blame the other, meaning that they each naïvely assume that if the other would just change, the conflict would disappear.

These simplistic answers do not come close to describing what is actually driving conflict. As conflict increases and does not get handled well, blame increases, criticism increases, and self-focus decreases. Partners tend to focus on the more negative traits of their partners and forget about the very things that attracted them in the first place. They begin using the word "you" constantly instead of examining what they might be contributing to the relationship problems. Narrowly focusing on what their partner is doing wrong means that couples end up feeling hopeless that they will ever resolve the conflict.

How did they get here, though? What happened to the fun at the beginning of the relationship? How did they end up in these escalating patterns of conflict? Understanding the underlying, and less simplistic/blame-ridden, reasons for conflict in relationships is essential.

Take a minute to think about the arguments you have with your partner. We typically have our favorite go-to topics that are guaranteed to spark conflict ... you know, the ones where you can say both your lines and your partner's verbatim. Think about the topics in the following list and others that may get you and your partner stuck:

- ❏ Kids and parenting
- ❏ Sex
- ❏ In-laws
- ❏ Money and finances
- ❏ Others: _____

_____
_____
_____
_____

The Problem is that You are Probably Focusing on the Wrong Problem

The problem with the list in the previous section is that most couples describe their problems in these terms, which are too concrete. They believe that if they could just rebalance their roles, or work together on financial planning, or agree on how to spend holidays, or resolve any number of other issues, they would be fine. As a result, couples come to therapy looking for solutions to these very specific problems. They naïvely believe that if they could figure out solutions to money, sex, or parenting issues, that they would stop arguing. In reality, they are focused on the wrong thing.

By focusing so narrowly on the specific problem, they miss the fact that **the way they are trying to solve the problem is really the problem**. Their solution to the initial problem has now become the problem itself. This means that their conflict is not about the content (sex, parenting, etc.), but it's about the process! As we said previously, this process is part of an intense emotional system that is larger than any individual issue a couple is trying to resolve.

In order to better understand the emotional system that a couple is a part of, we have to first understand a very important goal of the emotional system: the issues that couples are trying to solve are connected to the regulation of closeness and distance.

The Problem of Regulating Closeness and Distance

Marriage, and being part of being a successful couple, require the ability to negotiate closeness and distance (Bowen and Kerr, 1988). Marriage offers partnership, an end to loneliness, and the hope of deep connection, which is the good news. The bad news is that it also introduces the threat of the loss of self. Balancing closeness and distance is complicated, and more often than not, we marry someone who balances it very differently than we do. This means that the person who craves closeness tends to marry someone who needs more space or distance. This then begins a difficult, but necessary negotiation in order for both partners to feel comfortable and have their needs met. When this negotiation goes awry, the following interaction develops and then intensifies: the person craving more closeness pursues their partner and the person needing distance moves further away from their partner, which creates a cycle of interaction that typically makes the problem much worse. In the midst of this intense interaction, there is usually very little insight into the real source of the problem: how to find a successful resolution to the problem of balancing closeness and distance. For most couples, this is one of the deepest sources of conflict that <u>they don't even realize they are negotiating</u>.

In reality, most people balance the closeness/distance equation differently. Ask yourself:

❑ When you get anxious or upset, do you move toward people or away from people?

_____
_____
_____
_____
_____

❑ Do you want to talk things out right away and resolve the issues, or do you need space to think?

_____
_____
_____
_____
_____

Everyone has a default: some move towards people and others move away. This means that balancing closeness and distance is more complicated if you and your partner answer the questions differently. Too often, the attempt to find balance ends up creating a powerful interaction.

> When Bob says to his wife Sheila, "you never want to spend time with me; you are always preoccupied with the kids," Sheila of course gets defensive and fires back, "if you only helped more with the kids, there would be more time to hang out."

Bob and Sheila have played out this conflict many times. Not surprisingly, this discussion is rapidly going nowhere good, as it easily becomes intense, leaving both feeling more and more angry and misunderstood.

The balance of closeness and distance is one of the fundamental issues that every relationship must negotiate. This negotiation is complicated, though, because these issues often do not emerge in the dating period or early years of a marriage. When they eventually do emerge, partners end up saying unhelpful things like, "You have changed! You always wanted to talk and hang out. You are not the person I married." Then, to make matters worse, when one person pursues, the other begins to feel smothered, which makes them anxious and more withdrawn. The withdrawal triggers anxiety in the pursuer, causing them to feel abandoned, which creates even more anxiety and more pursuit ... which, as you might guess, does not impact the distancer well. We could keep going around and around (like couples do) until the intensity is so powerful that we've completely lost sight of everything else and are stuck in a seemingly senseless, and unending conflict.

Of course, as we've said, couples are not aware of the closeness/distance needs that they are trying to negotiate. This means that, in the midst of this highly anxious interaction, both partners are focused on the more surface issue: spending time together. Ultimately, they then miss the deeper issue that that they are struggling with, which is a universal marital problem: balancing closeness and distance, and how their differences in personality make that more complicated.

Think now about those concrete conflicts that you identified earlier. Reflect for a moment on how they interact with the questions you answered about your pursue/distance preferences.

❏ Think about the content of these conflicts (kids, in-laws, money, etc.) and how they relate to an underlying process of managing closeness and distance.

_____
_____
_____
_____
_____

- ❑ How can you talk about the same conflict without talking about the content, but rather the process underlying that content?

_____
_____
_____
_____
_____

- ❑ Can you link your points/focus in the conflict to a need related to closeness or distance?

_____
_____
_____
_____
_____

The Problem of Emotional Systems

A second contribution to conflict is that couples form an <u>emotional interactional system</u>, which is a mouthful! Simply stated, this means that <u>a couple's interactions are not driven by logic or reason, but instead by emotion</u>. Think again about regulating closeness and distance. An emotional interaction forms between a couple, which takes on a life of its own in an attempt to regulate closeness and distance. Let's play a little bit with your last fight – that one that got away from you where you regret some of (or maybe all of) what you said or did.

Think first about how this conflict started and how it escalated:

- ❏ Did it start on one topic?
- ❏ Did it become more emotional as the discussion went on?
- ❏ Did additional topics start getting added as the emotion intensified?
- ❏ Did the discussion get shut down as emotion started to get more intense?
- ❏ Was there a declaration made about ending the relationship? Or was there hopelessness that the conflict will ever have a resolution?

How did the argument get so "crazy", and how did you completely lose the point of the original topic? In reality, you would be embarrassed if your conflict were recorded and you had to watch it. Of course, the next day when you and your partner attempt to figure out what went wrong, neither of you can even remember how the conflict started, much less how it got away from you. You are left physically and emotionally exhausted, discouraged, and confused. That is the power of an emotionally driven interaction!

> Diane and John – two very bright professionals – sit dejected and feeling hopeless as they describe, with a sense of resignation and despair, how their conflicts take off quickly and powerfully. They are both confused about how these conflicts happen, and they talk about how they are more than capable of problem solving in

Renewing your Relationship

their professional lives without being reactive. In fact, they each solve problems creatively for a living! They cannot understand how things go so wrong between them, though. Diane states with frustration: "I just talked about how I feel alone with the kids and how I need more help. The next thing I know, John is saying that I don't understand how much pressure he is under at work, and how I'm making him feel like a terrible husband!"

John responds defensively, "I'm sick of feeling like everything I do does not measure up to your standards – you are impossible! And... you are just like your mother!" Of course, Diane is now hooked, and retorts, "You want to talk about family dynamics? Really? What about you and your father?"

With this exchange, John and Diane are now off and running, engaging in mutual attack and moving further away from their presenting problem. What they fail to understand, despite how articulate and intelligent they are in other aspects of their lives, is that the source of their conflict has very little to do with the content of their argument. Rather, it is tied to an "emotional system" that they have co-created. This system creates a feedback loop in which they become increasingly reactive and – however inadvertently – reinforce in the other the very thing they don't want. In so doing, Diane and John have created an interaction (see our description in book one, *Renewing Your Relationship: 5 Necessary Steps*) that rapidly takes on a life of its own. It is bigger than the sum of its parts, and they are unable to regulate this ever-escalating spiral of interaction and conflict. It can be likened to being trapped on a runaway train.

As we talked about in the first book, these interactional patterns have complementary feedback loops. This means that, without wanting to, couples reinforce the behaviors they dislike in their partners. For example, the **overfunctioner** "trains" their partner to underfunction, while the **underfunctioner** "forces" their partner to overfunction. Or, the **pursuer** inadvertently pushes their partner away, while their partner's withdrawal creates more pursuit. In both examples, feedback loops create a circular interactional pattern, where both are reinforcing the traits in their partner that they actually want to change. This feedback loop is powerful and, in the end, traps both parties in something that they cannot easily escape. Of course, these interactional cycles have fuel – anxiety – to keep them powered. The greater the anxiety, the more intense interactions become. This is because anxiety does not make us more creative or smart, but, in reality, anxiety makes us dumb! This means that anxiety driven interactions will always go badly. (Reread our first book for more information on the power of anxiety.)

The Problem Goes Deeper

Would you find it reassuring if we mentioned that your style of conflict makes sense? Everyone has an internal map, so to speak, for handling conflict. These maps are rooted in experiences with the family you grew up in, and we are often not aware of them. Every family, though, has a style of conflict. Some families, for example, are loud and noisy: they yell at each other, become very emotional, and then settle down and go on as if nothing happened. Somehow, this works for those families. At the other extreme, some families are very conflict-avoidant and polite, which means that conflict (even though it's definitely there) rarely surfaces. If two people (one from each of these style families) marry, they are going to have difficulty because their conflict styles are completely opposite. Both will assume, of course, that the style they adapted from their family is normal and healthy. However, when these two styles are blended, nothing will ever get resolved and both will assume that the other's style is the problem and needs to change.

Too often, couples don't know that they need to compare their "conflict maps" and how they were shaped by their families of origin as well as by early experiences.

To handle conflict creatively:

1. Each individual must know what their conflict map is.

2. Couples need to compare these maps.

3. Couples need to begin to build a joint map, that integrates the styles and needs of each, for handling conflict.

If these steps do not happen, couples are operating with two very outdated GPS systems that give different directions related to navigating conflict, which only maintains and further intensifies the conflict.

Of course, navigating conflict becomes more complicated with individuals who grew up in families with alcoholism, addiction, or in families where anger eventually turned to violence. People who grew up in these families may have been traumatized by the power of explosive, alcohol-fueled anger and learned to shut down or become peacemakers in order to stay safe. As a result, anger is seen as extremely dangerous, and they tend to see conflict as something to be avoided at all costs for fear of re-experiencing the trauma they grew up with. Often, these individuals have difficulty even expressing what they need for fear of triggering conflict, since they learned as children to be peacemakers. As such, these people unconsciously decided to try to be as "invisible" as possible, and to have no needs, and their adaptive defenses kept them safe. In reality, however, these defenses no longer work for them, but instead work against them. Working hard to make peace or avoid anger costs these people greatly when it comes to their personal needs, as well as their need for intimacy in their primary relationships.

Dawn describes tearfully how, during her childhood, her father would begin drinking before dinnertime and would become progressively more intoxicated. She recalls sitting at the table feeling anxious and tense, trying to keep everyone calm. She would never dream of expressing any feelings, and she remembers working hard to control the conversation so that her father would not get upset. She dreaded how the evening would progress, often ending in a screaming match between her parents, during which she would try to console her younger siblings. Now, as an adult, she struggles to ever share what she needs with her husband, and consistently shuts down conflict for fear of where it could go. Intellectually, she knows there is no present threat, but still cannot face any type of conflict without getting extremely tense.

In much the same way, children who were never securely attached to their parents as safe and nurturing caregivers are afraid that anger could cause greater loss. To have needs, to express those needs, and to move closer to being assertive with those needs is to risk losing even more security with those they love. They believe that if they have very few needs they might actually be loved, so they avoid conflict and tend to overfunction in the hope of feeling loved.

All of these experiences growing up help form a map about how to do conflict, but all too often, these maps are not reflected on, discussed, or negotiated. Understanding these maps and how they formed, though, is central to dealing with conflict in a healthy way, and to increasing healthy intimacy.

Summary

To begin to better understand the real sources of conflict, we believe it is necessary to first look at what really drives conflict. We will describe in some detail different patterns for handling conflict later on, but first it is necessary to better understand the underlying causes of marital conflict. Ultimately, conflict is never about the "content" couples argue over, but rather about the negotiation of closeness and distance, which in turn traps couples in emotional interactions that are often fueled by anxiety. Finally, old family maps provide instructions for handling conflict.

To begin handling conflict in a healthier way, couples need to first wrestle with these deeper underlying issues. Without understanding these deeper issues, couples will make little progress, and will feel more stuck and hopeless with time. Unfortunately, this is when separation or divorce becomes likely. Hopefully, we can create the understanding that there may be ways to regain hope and make real shifts that make conflict solvable and increase intimacy.

Questions for Reflection

1. Do you move towards people or away from people when you are hurt or anxious?

2. Does your partner move towards people or away from people when they are hurt or anxious?

3. How do you, as couple balance, closeness and distance?

4. What is your internal map for handling conflict? How was it handled in your family of origin?

5. What does all of this mean about what conflict looks like in your relationship?

_____
_____
_____
_____
_____
_____
_____
_____
_____
_____
_____
_____
_____
_____
_____
_____
_____
_____
_____
_____
_____
_____

Chapter 2:
Conflict Styles that Prevent Intimacy

As we talked about in Chapter 1, every couple has a map for handling conflict, as well as an interactional pattern for managing conflict. To begin handling conflict differently, it is important to begin to recognize the pattern that you and your partner are using. Understand that your style of conflict becomes a pattern which takes on a life of its own, and in the end guarantees that problems will not be solved until the interaction is shifted.

Try to read this chapter with a focus on identifying your conflict style. You may find that you have different styles for different problems, which is ok. For example, you make be conflict avoidant about handling finances, but escalate rapidly when talking about in-laws. Read slowly and listen for yourself. (Remember: focus on you, not on your partner!)

The Conflict-Avoidant Couple
Trading Passion for Politeness

No one likes conflict. In fact, we have experienced couples coming in for sessions on a Friday asking to keep the session "light" so they could have a good weekend. But in reality, avoiding conflict can actually kill intimacy in marriage. Too often, couples who claim that they never fight also complain that they have no intimacy. Ironically, while avoiding conflict does make for polite relationships, it is also one of the biggest blocks to achieving deep intimacy; without realizing it, couples that avoid conflict have traded intimacy for politeness and distance. They may never fight, but they often do not share other emotions either. Theirs is a polite but distant relationship.

Typically, couples believe that they avoid conflict for very good reasons. They do not want to upset their spouse; they want to keep things calm; or it just takes too much energy. And sometimes they are not even clear about why they are avoiding conflict. Yet, in avoiding conflict, important issues will be driven underground and the pair will grow further apart.

Couples avoid conflict for a number of reasons. Perhaps they grew up in a high-conflict family where anger easily got out of control, and great damage was inflicted on everyone. If you grew up in this type of family, you will carry a type of hypervigilance that will make you want to avoid conflict at all costs. If you are hypervigilant you will find yourself always a bit tense, always anticipating problems, and rarely focused on your own needs or what you want and need from your partner. As we talked about previously, if there was alcoholism or substance abuse, it is even more complicated. Alcoholism can wreak havoc in families, leaving children frightened, insecure, and longing for peace and safety. So of course, they want desperately to stay away from conflict at any cost.

Others worry about their spouse: "If I am really honest, can s/he handle it?" They doubt that their partner will be able to cope with what is stirred up by their honest feedback. They believe that to keep the marriage stable, they have to be careful not to upset their spouse by talking about their frustrations or their needs. Instead, they keep things as calm as possible by not bringing up things that bother them. They are convinced that their partner cannot handle honest feedback or criticism.

Still others fear that their relationship is so fragile that if conflict surfaces, they will not be able to recover. These couples work hard to keep everything polite in order to protect their relationship. Couples avoid conflict because they are convinced that the alternative is too dangerous. Their strategy does work: things stay calm. In the end, however, this calmness comes with a hefty price tag—their intimacy.

Conflict-avoidant couples must keep interactions on the surface and find ways to keep things calm. To do this, they tend to focus on their kids, or their careers, or their friendship group. In the end, their connection is not based on anything real between the two of them, as both partners have difficulty expressing deep needs. These couples know something is missing but they are too anxious to begin talking about it because opening the potential conflict is too dangerous. Even when they finally go for couples therapy, they tend to "dance" around important issues and focus on minor issues. Like every other couple, their problem is co-created with their symmetrical dance. Both partners participate in avoiding conflict and keeping things calm because both are equally frightened that conflict will be destructive.

The Rapid Escalator Couple
Zero to Sixty in Ten Seconds

In contrast to conflict avoiders, rapid escalator couples are quite the opposite. Almost any topic can escalate and blow up for these couples. Like their name suggests, these couple conflicts escalate very quickly with more and more emotion until the argument is out of control and has little hope of resolution.

The conversation started innocently enough: Dan wanted Sarah to know that he was feeling overwhelmed with the level of responsibility he has around the house and with the kids, on top of working full time. He wanted her to pick up a few of the daily tasks so that he could balance his needs better. Not even five minutes later, Sarah is screaming about how Dan missed the family photo two months ago, Dan is accusing Sarah of being overly close to her parents... they are hurtling insults and condemnations back and forth, and neither has any clue how the whole mess of a conversation started, or how to slow it down.

Rapid escalation conflicts go from 0–60 quickly, meaning a couple starts by talking about a simple need or issue and ends by talking about five unrelated issues and then maybe separation and/or divorce as well. These couples are hijacked by the conflict style in a way that prevents any healthy conversation about their needs. In fact, "hijacked" is a good word for it because these couples are not conversing with one another in a logical manner any longer. Their brain's limbic systems (think amygdala and fight-or-flight response) have taken over. As Dan and Sarah know all too well, no good comes from a conversation that has been hijacked by the amygdala.

Once these couples are hijacked, their arguments are like a runaway train that gets away from them, leaving both feeling demoralized and hopeless. Rather than recognize that their dysfunctional dance is the problem and try to change it, they blame each other. As they continue to blame each other, the dance continues to get worse, which adds to their hopelessness.

The Partner Who Gives Up Self to Avoid Conflict
"I'll Have What He's (or She's) Having"

Similar to conflict-avoidant couples, this style keeps conflict shut down by virtue of one partner giving up, or sacrificing, their own needs and wants for the sake of calm. In this case, however, the dance is not symmetrical like the conflict-avoidant couples' dance. Here, one person makes a decision (often unconsciously) to keep things calm by giving up their needs. Their partner, then, has their needs met at the sacrifice of the first's needs.

The partner who gives up self frequently grew up as the overfunctioner in an alcoholic or dysfunctional family, where they attempted to stabilize their family by being "needless" and providing for the family's needs. This was typically the child who was responsible for everything, and as a result did not have the space to think about what they needed. Their partners, on the other hand, are more likely to have grown up in families that were over-responsive or over-protective. Alternatively, they may also have grown up in a family that was equally disorganized, but not as the overfunctioner. Rather, their role may have allowed them to define their needs, but not have their needs met, creating a strong longing to find someone who could take care of them. The dance these two then create is powerful.

From the outside, these marriages appear healthy, and they are calm and peaceful. The "health" of these marriages, however, is contingent on one partner denying their own needs (if they even know what those needs are) for the sake of taking care of their partner, who appears weak or needy. This means that conflict is never processed because the one who denies their own needs believes their partner cannot cope with conflict and will not manage their own feelings and reactions.

These relationships typically begin to come apart when the partner who gives up self experiences physical and/or emotional symptoms. Frequently, the overfunctioning partner develops headaches, stomach problems, frequent illnesses, anxiety, depression, or sleep disturbances. This is the price of giving up too much self to keep the relationship stable. Thus, in the end, these peaceful marriages are fundamentally unbalanced, and are not able to handle conflict or achieve intimacy.

The Passive Aggressive Partner
"Why Are You Getting So Upset?"

This conflict style is seen in the following interaction:

Mary calmly said to her husband George, "You seem angry," to which George replied, "I'm fine. I'm not angry at all." George then promised his wife he would be willing to talk more later. When later came, George "forgot" about talking more and fell asleep watching TV. When Mary confronted him the next morning, he replied defensively, "Give me a break! I'm exhausted and just fell asleep," but then he ignored her for several days after.

Welcome to the world of the passive aggressives! These couples are beyond difficult to deal with and are rarely able to resolve conflicts. There are similarities between the passive aggressives and the conflict avoiders, but the distinguishing mark of a passive aggressive is that they are very angry at their partners. Unfortunately, their anger comes out indirectly by "forgetting" that they were going to watch a movie, or falling asleep when they were going to talk, or by losing interest in sex. They often procrastinate or run late, and they withhold affection and use sarcasm while they pretend it's humor.

Passive aggressives use a number of key phrases including, "I'm not angry", "Ok - Fine!", "I was only joking", "Don't be so sensitive", or "Don't worry, I'll get to it later."

Because passive aggressives refuse to admit to their anger, they make their partners feel as if they are the only ones with the problem. Worse still, when their partner gets angry, they act confused. It can truly be crazy making!

A variation of this pattern is the "yes dear, whatever you say" style. One defers to the other, but in the end is left feeling angry and resentful, and pulls further away creating significant distance in the relationship. As one man said in my office, "when my wife is upset, I just nod my head and agree". Of course, his wife will pay for it later.

Ultimately, this style is a way to cover deep hostility, while at the same time avoiding dealing with the anger. They deny the anger to themselves and to their partners, and then "passively" punish their partners who feel like they are going crazy. This style represents a deep fear of conflict, and even of one's own anger. Passive aggressives can be quite punitive, and, in the end, they have a deadly way of handling conflict that destroys any possibility of intimacy.

The Fight/Withdraw Combination Couple
Constant Hide and Seek

This pattern is a complicated pattern to track. Unlike the conflict avoidant and rapid escalator couples, in which both partners use the same style for handling conflict, these couples use opposite styles. Here, one partner moves toward the other with what they need, or with a complaint, and the other partner responds by shutting down. The person initiating the conflict is now frustrated and pushes the conflict, but this just makes their partner more upset, which causes further withdrawal. The pursuer may give up for some time, feeling both resentment and deep frustration. Eventually, though, they end up so frustrated that they blow up in anger, which then leaves their partner convinced that conflict really is dangerous. This couple, then, can never solve anything or move toward intimacy.

What Is Your "Fighting Style"?

In order to begin shifting your pattern of handling conflict so that you and your partner can solve the issues and begin to move toward greater intimacy, begin by reviewing the patterns described in this chapter. Which patterns best describe your style of handling conflict with your partner? Are you able to identify multiple patterns that you relate to depending on what the conflict is about?

Part of creating change is understanding what conflict style you use for which problems so that you can gain clarity into that pattern. Of course, the most difficult part of this is to not focus on your partner, but instead focus on yourself and what you do in the midst of conflict.

Questions for Reflection

In order to improve the way you handle conflict, review these patterns and ask yourself these questions:
1. What pattern do you and your partner typically use when conflict arises?

2. What is your role in the conflict? Pretend someone has recorded the conflict - what would you notice about what you do? How do you respond to your partner? How do you (or don't you) understand and regulate your own emotional response?

3. Are you able to recognize a pattern of handling conflict that goes back to your childhood?

4. The next time conflict arises in your relationship, work on recognizing when you start to become caught up in your conflict pattern, and catch it <u>before it gets away from you</u>.

_____
_____
_____
_____
_____
_____
_____
_____
_____
_____
_____
_____
_____

Chapter 3:
Breaking Your Conflict Pattern

At this point, you are more aware of your pattern for handling conflict and the ways in which it is not working well. You want to make some changes now, but the question is where to begin. Changing an entrenched pattern can be difficult, but there is hope. More often than not, what you say and do in conflict is predictable, which is actually helpful here. If you tend toward a conflict avoidant style, you most likely get tense as conflict begins and then look for ways to close it down. If you give away self to stabilize the relationship, you probably pay careful attention to what your partner says or does, and tune into their reactions while tuning out what you are feeling. Then, you calibrate your reaction in accordance with how they act. If, on the other hand, you are part of a rapid escalator couple, you will notice yourself quickly getting agitated, and wanting to attack as opposed to listening or understanding.

The objective of this chapter is to enable you to break your accustomed patterns of behavior by using the following process. In step 1, you identify the general pattern of conflict that you and your partner use, and identify your role in that pattern; in step 2, you and your partner learn how to read your individual 'conflict maps' and understand the reasons behind their development.

Step 1: Identifying Your Pattern of Conflict

Step one in changing your pattern of conflict—identifying your pattern of conflict—is both the easiest and most obvious, and it has two phases: First, recognizing the pattern; and second, identifying the part you play in that pattern.

Phase 1: Recognizing Your Conflict Pattern

To help with the first phase, look over the conflict patterns that we described in the last chapter, and see if you recognize your pattern. Try to first identify the pattern that best illustrates how you and your partner handle conflict in general. As we also suggested, ask yourself if the pattern changes as you change the problem you are working on.

Phase 2: Identifying Your Role in Your Pattern

The second phase is a little trickier for most to do. It is one thing to describe your conflict pattern: it is easy to recognize rapid escalation or conflict avoidance. You might even be able to describe a typical argument and see how it fits into one of those patterns. **The most challenging part of this next step, though, is to just look at your part in the interaction or argument.** Think back on your last conflict. How did it start? How did it build? Now step back and just look at your role in the conflict.

Confused? OK - pretend you are watching a video of the conflict between you and your partner in slow motion. Watch carefully, only studying yourself and your reactions and think through this again:

1. What are you feeling as the conflict starts?

   ❏ Anxious? Agitated? Frustrated? Defensive?

   _____
   _____
   _____
   _____
   _____

2. Once you know what you feel at the start, what do you say and do next?

   ❏ Do you shut down or attack or immediately become defensive?

   _____
   _____
   _____
   _____
   _____

   ❏ Do you listen to what your partner says, or are you already rehearsing what you are going to say in response?

   _____
   _____
   _____
   _____
   _____

Most people naturally focus on their partner and their partner's contribution, and then see themselves as an "innocent victim" of their partner's reactions or issues. It is far more helpful, though, to begin by just looking at yourself and your own contribution. Doing so allows you to focus on changing your contribution—which is, after all, the only thing you can really change. So, carefully study what you do in the midst of conflict. In part, you will do this when you look back on previous conflicts and begin to recognize what was happening for you. It is also important, however, to track your own internal and external reactions as a conflict begins and continues. Focus on what you are feeling at the beginning of the conflict, notice what you say and do, notice the impact of what you say and do on your partner, notice how they react, and then notice how you react to their reaction. You can learn quite a bit from this exercise if you can slow down and focus on yourself.

> Jan was surprised when she watched herself carefully. Typically, she blamed Ralph, her husband, for his high level of frustration and agitation with her and tried to get him to go for therapy to get a better handle on his agitation. However, when she watched herself carefully (with the help of some feedback from her friends) she was surprised to see how she constantly interrupted Ralph, finished his sentences, and corrected his thoughts. She began to slowly understand that this habit agitated him, and realized that she was, at least in part, creat-

ing the anger and agitation in Ralph that she was constantly critical of. For Jan, this was an important recognition. Not surprisingly, when she shifted her style and stopped interrupting, her husband's agitation decreased.

Step 2: Learning and Understanding Your Conflict Map

Step two in changing your pattern of conflict learning and understanding your (and your partner's) conflict map—goes a little deeper. Before you can try to make practical steps toward change, you need to understand that your conflict style is what it is for a reason. Truthfully, so is your partner's. There is always a logic to why we do what we do and why we handle conflict the way we do: Whether we know it or not, we have internalized a map. This map has "helpful" hints for how to handle conflict, and informs your beliefs about conflict itself, anger, your partner, and even about yourself. While this map sounds helpful, it can actually make conflict much more complicated: unless you unpack these core beliefs and examine them, you and your partner will find it very difficult to shift your conflict style.

Patterns of Conflict are Rooted in Beliefs about Conflict, and They Make Sense!

First - start by reflecting on what you really believe about conflict. Is conflict inherently dangerous? Will conflict always lead to serious marital problems? Will you be heard if you do not speak loudly and with anger? Or do you believe good marriages are conflict free and that good marriage is always smooth sailing? These beliefs are part of your "conflict map", which are rarely reflected on, even though they form a strong internal GPS which automatically takes over when conflict starts. This means that not exploring your core beliefs about conflict and anger will cause your conflict GPS to take over, automatically shifting you into a patterned way of handling conflict. Although your conflict style may not be working well relationally, it does make sense: if you believe conflict is inherently harmful, this GPS will respond, and automatically shut things down and try to make peace and avoid difficult topics. Unfortunately, this has the consequence of shutting down intimacy automatically too.

Second - ask yourself what your beliefs about your partner and conflict are. Try to go with the first uncensored response that comes to mind about your partner. Do you dread conflict with them because you believe they will be too reactive or explosive? Do you avoid conflict with them because they get so intense that you end up feeling defensive and then shut down to try to "put the fire out"? Or are you afraid that if you bring anything up, they will be very wounded or oversensitive? These pictures will have a powerful impact on how you handle conflict.

> John, for example, states that he "walks on eggshells" around his wife and fears that

if he brings up anything too controversial she will "blow up" and become highly emotional.

Marge, on the other hand, believes that her husband is too intense, and when they get into conflict, his intensity creates so much anxiety in her that she inevitably shuts down.

Angela states that when she challenges her husband about how little he does around the house, he becomes wounded and sulks for days claiming, "you must think I'm a terrible husband", and then can get depressed.

Given the beliefs these individuals have of their partner, they will most likely avoid conflict. There are similar ways of understanding the rapid escalators and overfunctioners as well. These beliefs we have of our partners have a huge impact on how we process conflict.

To begin to make changes, start by asking yourself the following questions:

❏ What do I really believe about conflict?

_____
_____
_____
_____
_____

- ❏ Is conflict healthy or unhealthy?

___

- ❏ Does conflict lead to intimacy and a deeper relationship, or does it destructively tear people apart?

___

- ❏ Do I try to avoid conflict?

___

- ❏ What am I most afraid of about conflict?

___

- ❏ If you get overly angry or sensitive about conflict, ask: What beliefs do I hold that could be driving this style?

_____
_____
_____
_____
_____

- ❏ What do I believe about my partner and conflict?

_____
_____
_____
_____

- ❏ Can my partner tolerate my feelings?

_____
_____
_____
_____

- ❏ Is my partner safe and trustworthy with their feelings and reactions?

_____
_____
_____
_____

Beliefs Get Reinforced by Feedback Loops

Conflict becomes further complicated since, inevitably, couples create feedback mechanisms where they actually reinforce their partner's beliefs, both about conflict and about themselves.

> Angela, who we just mentioned, believes her partner cannot handle any criticism, so she does her best to hold back. At the same time, she resents that she gets very little help with the kids and the house. To keep things calm, she overfunctions and doesn't ask for much help. Finally, she gets exhausted and explodes saying, "I can't do it anymore! I'm exhausted and overwhelmed and you don't care enough to help. I'm so sick of your selfishness!" Her husband, Dan, did not see this coming and, of course, is extremely defensive and responds just as she expected he would saying, "so I'm just worthless".

Without meaning to, Angela set her husband up to be defensive. Rather than talking when she was calm and thinking about how she wanted to express her concerns, she waited until she was exhausted and then blew up and "dumped" all the frustration that she had been holding for months. Of course Dan was going to react badly! Unfortunately, though, Dan's reaction confirmed Angela's belief that he cannot handle criticism. This then caused Angela to vow not to bring anything up in the future, and to suck it up and continue to overfunction. Dan, on the other side, is left with the anxiety that, down deep, Angela does not see him as a good husband. He will briefly try to make a few changes, but soon things will go back to the way they were. Both have reinforced the other's picture, causing them to remain stuck in their unhelpful conflict style.

All conflict gets caught in familiar feedback loops, which quickly reinforce the way couples see one another. At the end of the conflict, both have further locked in their core beliefs about conflict itself, and about their partner. These feedback loops cement negative conflict styles in place making them very difficult to change.

How We See Ourselves Influences Our Conflict Style

Finally, patterns of conflict are also reinforced by deeply held **beliefs we have about ourselves**, which are not often conscious. For example, if you carry shame - a deep sense of your own defectiveness or unworthiness - you will not move toward being assertive or taking the risk of conflict in order to get your needs met because of the fear of others seeing your defectiveness. It's all too easy to neglect your needs in order to focus on the needs of those around you in the hopes of keeping the peace, and keeping your secret that at your core, you're worthless.

Conversely, if your needs never got met as child you may have developed a sense of "negative entitlement", meaning you may demand your partner in the present meet needs that were never met growing up. In case you were wondering, this doesn't usually go well. If those needs are not met, you may even become emotionally reactive.

Beliefs are Rooted in Family History

The last stop on our belief tracking expedition is family. Most of us developed a model for handling conflict based on what we observed growing up. If your family's style of conflict was destructive, or even violent, you have most likely learned to avoid conflict and attempt to placate your partner to avoid the type of chaos you experienced growing up. This means that you will automatically give up self in to make peace, and to keep from replicating your childhood. Your core belief that conflict is dangerous was formed for good reason!

Other families modeled the opposite. They modeled a belief that conflict is unnecessary and is an indication of an unhealthy relationship. These families are polite, and they seem healthy on the surface. However, no real issues ever get talked about or resolved, which results in problems.

Ethnicity is also an important factor to understand. Certain ethnic backgrounds can be more expressive and colorful, while other ethnic backgrounds can be quite reserved. Imagine an expressive Italian husband who grew up in a warm, but loud and argumentative family. He married a reserved woman from an English background whose family prided themselves on always being polite and restrained. This couple has to talk about their conflict styles, beliefs, and origins of those beliefs if they hope to ever resolve anything or have any level of intimacy.

Finally, **avoid the gender trap!** Men are NOT from Mars, and women are NOT from Venus, despite the popular book series by that title. In fact, forming a rigid and stereotypical gender-based picture of your partner will only make resolving conflict and finding intimacy more difficult. It is much more helpful to simply explore what both of you believe about conflict, what you learned from your families, and explore the ways you see each other.

While no one can argue that your beliefs about conflict while growing up were not accurate, we can argue that they are outdated and, therefore, unhelpful. Whatever the style, the importance of asking yourself what you learned from your family about conflict and how your beliefs developed cannot be understated when it comes to changing these patterns.

You Carry Patterns Internally That You May Not Be Aware Of

Just understanding the patterns of conflict in your family is a good start, but it is far more complicated than that in reality. For better or worse, we have internalized our families and their conflict patterns without realizing it.

> Susan for example, still finds herself getting anxious when her husband or co-workers get agitated. She understands intellectually that

there is no danger and that there is no reason to get so anxious, yet she can't help the anxiety. Susan grew up with a violent father who could easily, and unpredictably, become explosive over very minor things. She has vivid memories of her father hitting her younger siblings when he was enraged, and of trying to get him to stop. To try to avoid this, she attempted to be the peacemaker by trying to keep everyone calm. This meant that, in an attempt to make sure her father was in a good mood and to avoid violence and yelling, Susan never disagreed. In the present, Susan knows, intellectually, that her husband is not at all like her father, but when she senses he is in a bad mood, she instantly attempts to make sure he is ok, and shuts down what she needs for fear of upsetting him.

For Susan, her family history lives inside of her in a powerful way, and it takes over her reactions in her relationships. Insight alone is not enough here.

Questions for Reflection

Ask yourself and your partner the following questions to begin to understand more about your own internal family and mapping system:

- ❑ Did you learn to dread conflict because of violence or the threat of violence?

- ❏ Did you learn that conflict is unnecessary or unhealthy?

- ❏ Did you learn to swallow anger like your parents did, until it leaks in unhealthy ways?

- ❏ What was modeled for you about resolving problems?

Chapter 4:
Beginning to Make Change: From Conflict to Greater Intimacy

To begin the process of making change, you must first accept a vital and necessary premise: healthy conflict will lead to greater intimacy. Of course, the opposite is also true: conflict handled poorly will destroy intimacy and closeness. The second premise that you must accept is that you can only change yourself. As much as you'd like to change your partner, trying to do so will prove futile.

With these two truths as the foundation, we can begin to build toward change. In the last chapter, we suggested that you start by recognizing the style of conflict you use in most arguments. Next, recognize your role in the conflict, and how you either make that conflict better or worse. Third, identify your beliefs about conflict, as well as your beliefs about your partner. Finally, recognize where those beliefs come from as you explore the impact of your family of origin. This is the beginning of change.

Change does not happen just by thinking about these patterns and recognizing your role, however. Once you're able to answer the questions in the previous chapters about the above areas for exploration, you can begin to make steps toward changing patterns. To change your conflict pattern, there are a few principles and techniques that you will need in order to be successful.

Healthy Conflict Must Start Slow

As we've said in many different ways, conflict cannot go well if it is not handled in a non-reactive manner. This means that you cannot jump in hot and ready to debate or take your partner on. If you try this, the results will be the same as each time you've attempted to solve this conflict before. In reality, though, many arguments start hot! Too often, people save up resentments until they are ready to burst. When they start the discussion, then, they are already irritated, frustrated, and angry, meaning that they have waited too long. When they finally do express what they are feeling, they are already too agitated and angry, so their partner naturally becomes defensive very quickly.

Starting slow and soft is key to creating change, because when the interaction is moving too quickly and reactively, there is no room for greater self-awareness or for doing something different. While starting slow sounds good in theory, though, it is actually quite difficult to do. To start slow, make sure that you are not beginning an argument when you are already highly emotional, tired, or feeling triggered. Further, don't get into a conflict if there is alcohol involved or if it's late at night, as it will always go badly. Instead, try the following techniques to help keep the pace of the conflict slow:

First - as we've said previously, always begin talking about conflict when you are calm, not when you are angry, because no one benefits from beginning an argument when they are seething with pent-up frustration. Though this may seem to be the most obvious piece of advice in this list, it is the one least often followed. So, while the idea sounds good, in reality it is far from simple.

We know that most conflicts start with an explosion. Frustration has been saved up, and a bank account of bitterness has accumulated, and like a pressure cooker, the lid blows. This means that the argument begins from the amygdala, not the prefrontal cortex. As we explained in our first book, the amygdala is very limited in its responses: fight, flight, or freeze. These are the worst conditions under which to initiate conflict if you expect to be heard.

Instead, rather than yielding to the temptation to give in to what you are feeling and starting an argument when you are tired or totally frustrated, wait until you are more in control, and then start slowly. Wait until you are more in control, and then start slowly. It is so much better to calm yourself before opening conflict by thinking about the feelings before expressing them. Before blurting out what you are frustrated with, breathe, slow down, start soft.

Second - begin with an "I statement" that is reflective of what you are feeling and thinking. Do not attack or put your partner on the defensive: simply state what you want and need. For example, a conversation may start like this: "I have been very overwhelmed this last month or so, and I would like some more help with parenting the kids." Be careful not to make a black-and-white statement like "I'm so sick of doing everything, and you doing nothing", or name call, or make personal attacks.

Make sure you are being specific about what you want. After starting with an "I"-statement, be clear about what you are asking for by describing the behavior, how it makes you feel, and the change you want to see. You are not asking for a personality change; rather, you are asking for a specific change. So, instead of saying, "I'm sick of you not helping me", try "Would you help by putting the kids to bed with me every night", or "would you help me by taking responsibility for helping the kids with their homework". Be specific and ask for concrete changes.

Third - take responsibility for keeping the discussion on track. Too often when conflict escalates, multiple topics are thrown into the mix, emotions escalate, and phrases like "you always", "it must be nice to be perfect", "you never" get introduced. All of this intensifies both the emotion and the argument and guarantees that nothing will be resolved, and that both partners will feel even more distant.

To continue with our example, if you state "I have been very overwhelmed this last month or so, and I would like some more help with parenting the kids", and your partner generalizes with statements like "so you're saying I'm a terrible husband?" bring the discussion back to a specific concern by saying, "No, I think you are wonderful husband, but I would like more support with parenting our children." Be in charge of not letting the conflict escalate by keeping the discussion focused.

Anticipate that your partner will get defensive, since that is the most natural thing in the world. If you can anticipate the defensiveness, you can continue to bring the discussion back to what you want. Do not allow yourself to get reactive, but continue to bring the discussion back to the specifics of what you want and need.

Shannon had been feeling suffocated by Mike lately and was struggling with asking for space without causing him to feel rejected. Shannon started the conflicts well, stating "I don't feel like I am able to focus on the things that I enjoy doing separate from you. I'd like to take some more time to focus on my hobbies instead of watching movies with you each night." Initially, even though Shannon was starting calm and making I statements, their conversations derailed quickly as Mike's sense of being rejected caused him to react to feeling hurt in a defensive way, typically stating something to the effect of "you don't love me anymore." Of course, this triggered defensiveness in Shannon as well; the conflict began to devolve, and nothing was solved. Once Shannon recognized her ability to maintain control of her emotions and focus on the issue, she was able to change the script. When Mike responded defensively, Shannon was ready and was able to say, "I love you very much, and my desire to have a little more time to focus on my hobbies has nothing to do with me loving you less. I don't want to stop watching movies with you either, I just need a little more balance in our time together and apart." Mike was still a bit hurt and defensive, but Shannon maintained this focus on what she was asking for, and Mike felt more reassured and then able to balance what Shannon was asking for by agreeing to some time apart.

Fourth - If you find yourself getting sped up, even after a conflict starts well, and generalizing, blaming, or getting overwhelmed, feel free to call a time-out and calm down before returning to the conversation. If you are emotionally overwhelmed, or intensely agitated, continuing the conversation is bound to go badly.

In order to call a time-out, you must be able to recognize when you are triggered. Do you noticing your speech speeding up? Are you already rehearsing what you are going to say in response to what your partner is stating without really listening? Are your responses getting tense and beginning to attack?

If so, state: "I'm starting to get defensive and struggling to listen. Let's take a break and come back to this another time because I really want to understand your perspective." Then break cleanly, with no "last words."

Fifth - Finally, take an exploratory approach to hearing your partner rather than a "knowing" approach. This means that you'll want to ask a lot of questions and assume that you do not know the answers or your partner. Of course, you may hear what you expect, but at the very least this approach keeps the conversation calm. At best, you learn something new about your partner or you learn to see them a little differently. Whenever we feel like our partner really wants to understand our perspective, we tend to relax a little bit, which creates more potential to help the conflict.

Ground Rules for Conflict

As you practice these techniques, you will begin to observe patterns and areas where you and your partner get stuck. Observe where these techniques break down and, when things are calm, try to negotiate some ground rules to keep conflict on track. For example, if you observe that your worst arguments happen after 11:30 at night when you are both exhausted, try to avoid late-night discussions, and bring up issues earlier. If you notice that alcohol is always involved in your conflicts, make sure neither of you has been drinking before initiating a conflict. Exhaustion and alcohol consumption always escalate any conflict, making it far worse!

Remember, all good boxing matches, unlike street fights, have ground rules. There are places you hit, and places you don't, there are timed rounds, there is a ref, and there is a ring that contains the match. Likewise, all good conflicts need ground rules. Here are a few for starters:

- Stay on topic without generalizing to multiple topics

- No name calling
- Avoid attacking
- Recognize when you are getting defensive and take a time out
- Be careful with topics that you have been avoiding - they will fester under the surface, becoming more toxic with time
- Be aware of these buried resentments so they don't all come rushing out

Making Effective Repair

Always make repair. John Gottman's research (Gottman, 1999) suggests healthy couples have conflict, but always make repair. This is essential to their health and intimacy. Couples who believe that time will heal are, in the end, hurting themselves and losing intimacy in their relationship. Repair means checking in with your partner the next day by saying, "Last night we had a difficult conversation... I want to make sure you are OK and check in to see if we need more discussion. I want to make sure we both feel understood."

These check-ins are essential. Too often, couples are afraid that if they check in, then the fight or argument will start over again. In reality, though, the opposite is true. When arguments are not repaired, the unresolved feelings fall into the "bag of resentments" that too many people carry. As a result, the intensity of this resentment will increase over time, and at some point in the future, it will build to the point where all of these arguments will come pouring out.

Questions for Reflection

Ask yourself and your partner the following questions to begin to understand more about changing the way you manage conflict:

- ❏ What keeps you from starting conflict slowly – the triggers that you know will cause the pace to take off?

- ❏ What physiological signs do you recognize that tell you that you are feeling triggered?

- ❏ How can you take responsibility for the conflict pattern rather than letting it take you over?

- ❏ How can you better see your partner as someone who you do not completely know, but are open to knowing?

_____
_____
_____
_____
_____
_____
_____

Chapter 5: Making Real Lasting Change

Hopefully, at this point, you have become clear both on your pattern of conflict with your partner, and your role in the conflict. Maybe you have even had some success in shifting the pattern. More than likely, though, you are realizing how difficult it is to create change that endures, and how easy it is to get hooked back into the old pattern, and at times you may be feeling discouraged about making lasting change.

To move forward, ask yourself what you think the block to change is and why change is so difficult. There are several key blocks you should stay aware of: read on to see them.

Five Blocks to Making Lasting Progress
Block #1: The Problem of Anxiety

If we were able to stay cognitive and calm during conflict, there would be very little problem. Most people could then implement the techniques we have talked about this this workbook and see their conflicts resolve and their intimacy increase. Unfortunately, however, when conflict begins and builds, it is easy to get hijacked by the primitive part of the brain. As we explained in our previous book *Renewing your Relationship,* conflict triggers the emotional part of the brain—the amygdala.

The amygdala has a very limited repertoire of responses (fight, flight, or freeze) because it is meant to do one thing—react to what the individual perceives to be a dangerous situation. Obviously, the amygdala's responses do not lead to effective problem solving. Worse still, the amygdala triggers an adrenaline surge, which puts us in a state of hyperarousal, adding unnecessary fuel to an already tenuous conflict. When the conflict is getting out of control, this is an indication that you have been hijacked by your amygdala, which means that you are no longer capable of rational thinking. Remember, anxiety makes us dumb and dramatically limits our capacity for creative problem solving!

Learn to listen to your body! If your chest is tightening, or you are getting a headache, or you are no longer listening to your partner, but are already rehearsing what you are going to say in response—you have been hijacked. This is especially true if you have a history of trauma or grew up in a family where there was violence. That history can easily intensify your emotional reaction.

If you know you have been hijacked, try to focus on slowing down your breathing—and above all, stop talking! Use simple de-escalation phrases like "I'm going to shut up for a minute. Help me understand what I'm not understanding from your perspective. Help me get it."

If that is not effectively slowing the conflict down, ask for a brief time-out. Take a walk, go to another room: Let things slow down. <u>When anxiety has taken over, the most important thing is to not make things worse</u>.

Block #2: The Problem of the "Bitterness Bank"

If there is a history of unresolved conflict, or a tendency for conflict to go "underground," it is easy to build a bank account of bitterness and deeply held resentments. Unfortunately, this occurs far too easily in couples with poor conflict resolution skills. One result of this is that any conflict in the present can trigger a wave of old resentment, which can lead to a dumping of years of accumulated resentment. When this happens, the dumped-on spouse or partner has no idea what hit them, and they feel overwhelmed and hopeless. Naturally, this is destructive to the relationship and to intimacy.

If you are tired, or have been drinking alcohol, or are feeling very anxious, your normal filter will not be working well. This automatically opens the door to this destructive venting of bitterness. No matter what, try not to discuss these conflicts late at night or after you have been drinking. When your filter is not working, every resentment you have saved up may come tumbling out at once.

To handle conflict effectively, know what is in your bitterness bank: what are your resentments and old hurts? Once you clearly understand these old resentments and hurts, it becomes your responsibility to use discipline to keep the argument focused in the present, without dragging up history or old resentments. Dragging up old resentments will always escalate arguments, and make effective problem solving all but impossible.

Just as it is important that we work to not vent bitterness in destructive ways, it is equally important that we not let resentments build in the first place. This is particularly true if your style is conflict avoidant. If you ignore resentments to avoid conflict, the resulting accumulation of resentment and bitterness will grow like a cancer, endangering your relationship. Discipline yourself to break that pattern and address issues as they arise.

Block #3: The Problem of Forgiveness

Marriage is a wonderful laboratory for practicing forgiveness. At some point in every successful relationship, the decision is made to not allow the bitterness bank to build, but to move instead toward forgiveness. Ask yourself as you read on: Is there a way to put things in perspective and let go of old hurts and resentments?

To practice forgiveness, it is essential to understand that there are two levels of forgiveness. Level one means deciding not to hold "old debts" against your partner, and "collect interest" on old hurts or injuries. Forgiveness in this sense might mean to "cancel a debt." Level two is even more complicated as it means not only letting things go and not collecting interest, but also moving toward greater intimacy and vulnerability.

Part of what makes forgiving so difficult is that it leaves us so vulnerable. What if I forgive and get hurt again? What happens if I let go of my claim to collect interest—will my partner take advantage of me? Without increased vulnerability, though, there is no potential for resolution of conflict and increases in intimacy.

Many couples get caught in their cycle of conflict and pull out an old hurt to hit their partner with. For example, in the midst of an argument that begins getting out of control, Joan yells "I will never forgive you for the time ten years ago when you got drunk at our family Christmas party, and became insulting of me in front of my entire family. How can I ever trust you again?" Never mind that her partner has apologized numerous times and has taken responsibility for a drinking problem and addressed it: Joan still uses this example whenever an argument becomes intense. This is clearly a very destructive pattern, and in the end it powerfully escalates any argument, preventing focus, healthy solutions, and repair. At some point, Joan needs to make the decision to forgive. In this sense, forgiveness means letting it go, and consciously choosing to not keep bringing it up. Joan has to cancel the old debt. Obviously, this is extremely complicated. In the case of affairs or betrayals of any type, the issue must be adequately worked through, yes, but at some point forgiveness needs to be offered to allow the relationship to heal.

This is a complicated and important topic, often needing to be worked out with the help of a marital therapist. Forgiveness, in the end, is predicated on the fact that all problems are two-person problems and no one is entirely innocent. Even affairs do not happen in a vacuum. (For more information on forgiveness see Olsen's

The Spiritual Work of Marriage.) Ultimately, without forgiveness, the bitterness bank will continue to grow, and effective problem solving will be impossible. Allowing the bitterness bank to keep growing without forgiveness is a sure recipe for no intimacy in a relationship.

Block #4: The Problem of Self-Regulation

Self-regulation is central to the idea of both healthy marriage and conflict resolution. In our previous book, *Renewing your Relationship,* we began by suggesting that the only person you can really change is you, and ended the book with a final chapter on differentiation of self. Differentiation of self is the ability to "hold onto yourself" in the midst of an emotionally charged interaction with another, while still staying connected to the other. In other words, self-regulation is the ability to regulate what you are feeling while being emotionally engaged with your partner. Easier said than done, to put it mildly! Everything we have said about handling conflict, though, is contingent on being able to emotionally self-regulate.

What, Exactly, is Self-Regulation?

Self-regulation begins with self-awareness. This means that you know what you are feeling and thinking when conflict starts with your partner.

❑ What is happening in your body? (Remember what we said about the problem of anxiety.)

_____
_____
_____
_____
_____

- ❏ Are you getting tension in your chest, getting a headache, feeling like you are going to scream, getting a stomach ache?

_____
_____
_____
_____
_____

Use your body as a warning sign that you are getting too agitated. Then try to be clear what the feeling is:

- ❏ Are you hurt, frustrated, scared, or just plain angry?

_____
_____
_____
_____
_____

Understand what you are feeling and where it is coming from. As we said previously, it may be coming from your interpretation of what your partner is saying. It may come from feeling attacked, or from feeling misunderstood, or even from the accumulated data in the bitterness bank.

Now, don't stop at self awareness. Move from being aware of what you are feeling to better regulating what you are feeling. This may involve:

- ❏ Making sure you are expressing the right feeling; i.e. expressing hurt rather than anger.
- ❏ Thinking about what you are feeling before blurting it out.
- ❏ Choosing your words more carefully so you don't blurt too much out.
- ❏ Asking your partner if they feel like you are understanding their perspective before expressing what you are feeling.
- ❏ Slowing things down!! If you are feeling too much, take a break, go for a walk, but certainly do not take the risk of making things worse.

Finally, use your self-regulation to shift your part of the conflict cycle as we talked about in previous chapters. Recognize both the pattern of conflict and what your role is in the conflict, and then use your self-regulation skills to do something different. Remember, if you are successful in changing your role in this, your partner may very well try to pull you back into the old pattern. Be prepared for your partner to not be overly impressed when you change your role, and hold on anyway.

Block #5: The Problem of Empathy (or the Lack Thereof)

When couples struggle to resolve conflict, empathy becomes more difficult, making conflict and distance even worse. Empathy is the ability to connect to both what your partner is feeling and their subjective world, or the way they are seeing and understanding things. When we move to empathy, our partner feels understood, and escalations slow down. Understanding and empathic connection will always make problem solving easier, and help couples reconnect.

> Josh and Maria were in the midst of a very heated argument that was getting out of control. Both were getting hijacked and things were heading to the edge of the cliff. Suddenly, Maria slowed herself down, and to Josh's surprise said "I'm sorry! I know that when I'm hurt I attack and that is not fair to you. I have to work on expressing myself differently when I get hurt or scared." Josh instantly felt his anger drain, and his emotions soften. He was able to put his arms around his wife and feel both empathy and compassion. He remembered what she had had to deal with in childhood and was able to connect on a much deeper level. Not surprisingly, they were able to easily work through their conflict.

In the end, unresolved conflict erodes the capacity for empathy, and when empathy fades so does intimacy. The goal of self regulation and building conflict skills is not simply to better solve problems, but to increase empathy and therefore intimacy.

Summary

We have covered a lot of material about conflict. To help summarize, keep the following points in mind as you play with your own conflict style in your relationship:

1. Successful conflict resolution is necessary for an intimate relationship.

2. Conflict runs deeper than you think: it is often related to the problem of regulating closeness and distance and is made more complicated by patterned interactional cycles which become carefully scripted.

3. There are a variety of types of conflict patterns. By now you have hopefully been able to identify which pattern or patterns you and your partner use.

4. These patterns are grounded in your internal GPS. This is to say, you have a map for how to do conflict, grounded in pictures you have formed about both yourself and your partner, and at times grounded in beliefs you have about conflict itself.

5. These pictures, and your internal GPS, are often deeply rooted in family-of-origin history that we are frequently unaware of.

6. Finally, like everything, making change takes practice!! It will be awkward at first, but remember that insight does not produce change. Insight is simply the first step in creating change. It is imperative to understand your pattern and style of conflict, your pictures of yourself and your partner, and how that impacts conflict, not to mention how what you learned from your family of origin influenced your conflict skills.

7. The real work is changing yourself in the midst of conflict by learning to better self regulate and shift what you usually do as a step in changing the pattern of conflict. This is the beginning of change.

8. Remember, the only person you can ever change is you! By focusing on yourself, and changing your role, you are on the path to shifting the conflict pattern and deepening your relational intimacy.

Suggested Readings

Gottman, John. (1999). *The Marriage Clinic*. New York, NY: W. W. Norton & Company.

Kerr, Michael E., and Bowen, Murray. (1988). *Family Evaluation*. New York, NY: W. W. Norton & Company.

Olsen, David, and Belanger-Freeh, Erin. (2017). *Renewing Your Relationship: 5 Necessary Steps*. Denver, CO: Outskirts Press.